Are You a Boy or Are You a Girl?

by Sarah Savage and Fox Fisher

Jessica Kingsley Publishers
London and Philadelphia

My name is Tiny and this is my family.

We have just moved to a new town because Dad has a job as a bus driver.

We have a beautiful new house and
I will be going to a new school.

This is my bedroom in our new house.
Dad has built me a special bed that looks like a castle!

It's so big that I can keep all of my toys underneath and still have space to play with my little sister, Fiona.

Next to my bed are my fancy dress and toy boxes.

Dressing up is my favourite thing to do.

Fiona and I love to pretend we are animals or doctors, or even to host our own talent show.

"Tiny," asks Fiona, "are you a boy or are you a girl today?"

Mum lets us dress up whenever we want.

Today we are going to the park.

My sister is a cowboy and
I am dressed as a butterfly.

When we get home,
Dad is back from work
and is cooking dinner.

We are having spaghetti, my favourite!

Mum and I are getting my bag and clothes ready for the first day at school.

I hope I make some friends.

"Super Tiny, look! I've washed your favourite top for school tomorrow," Mum says.

The school is much bigger than my last one, but the teacher is very friendly and shows me where to sit.

The teacher tells the whole class, "It's Tiny's first day here so please be nice."

A boy shouts, "Tiny, what a silly name. I can't tell if it's a girl or a boy."

My new teacher says, "Buster, that's rude. Why does it matter if they are a boy or a girl?"

This morning is special because some firefighters are coming in to speak to us about fire safety.

"Girls can't be firefighters," Mia says.

But look, there is a lady driving the fire engine!

Later on we play football, my favourite.

Buster kicks the ball away and says, "Girls can't play football. It's for boys only."

Mia says, "I don't think it matters who plays, as long as we are all having fun."

Back in class, I draw a picture of Mia and Charlie for the school art show.

Buster spills my paint and laughs,
"Tiny is not a he. Tiny is not a she.

Tiny is an it!"

The teacher says, "Buster! Don't be a bully.
Why does it matter if Tiny is a girl or a boy?
Now say sorry and help Tiny tidy up."

"Sorry,"
says Buster.

"It's okay,"
I reply.

Tiny says, "What does it mean to be a boy or a girl?

I like eating cakes, playing football, dressing up and watching the stars."

"Oh...me too," says Buster.

After school, Charlie and Mia come over to my house to play with me and my new neighbour, Alfie.

We play in my bedroom, pretending
to be wild creatures.

Charlie is a crocodile, Mia is a tiger, Alfie is a fish and I am an owl.

As we are tidying up to get ready for dinner, Alfie asks me,

"Tiny, are you a boy or are you a girl?"

How are girls and
boys different?

Do you think that Tiny
is a boy or a girl?

Does it matter if Tiny
is a boy or a girl?

Should Tiny be allowed
to play football and
dress up as a fairy?

What would you ask
Tiny if you met them?

Would you like to
play with Tiny?

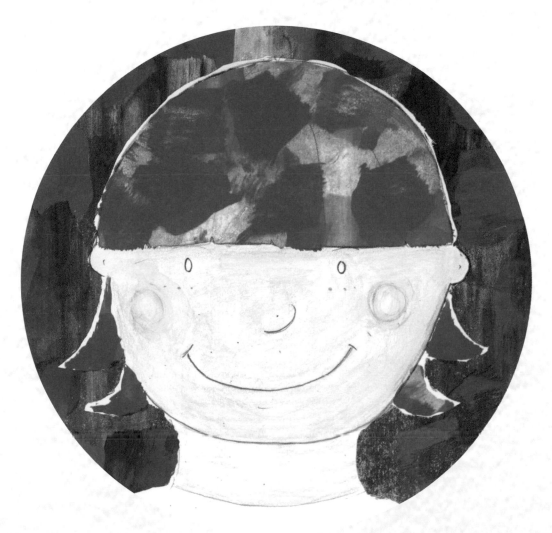

Gender Identity Research and Education Society (GIRES)

01372 801554
info@gires.org.uk
www.gires.org.uk

The focus of GIRES is on people who experience atypical gender identity development, especially trans people, whether or not they are also affected by Lesbian, Gay, Bisexual, Transgender or Intersex issues. This reflects the special interest of the trans people in the charity's membership. GIRES is concerned that society often treats this particular group harshly. This includes shortcomings in the provision of medical services.

www.mermaidsuk.org.uk

Mermaids is the only UK charity providing support for children and teenagers with gender identity issues and their families. Support is available via their helpline and online forums. Mermaids can help with many issues, including school, family and seeking treatment.

www.mygenderation.com

My Genderation is an ongoing film project used as a resource in the UK and beyond. Founded by Fox Fisher and Lewis Hancox, who met on documentary *My Transsexual Summer* (C4), and currently run by Fox and Owl, My Genderation remains made by trans people about trans people for a much wider audience.